KEY SKILLS
LEVEL 2

Survival Guide

Key Skills

Level 2

Application of Number

Sue Dent

20 01000 871

Contents

Choices

If you are just entering Year 10 or 11 at school, you will already have been making some important decisions about your future and how to prepare yourself for the time, even though it may be years ahead, when eventually you go to work. For example, studying languages or a science now may be the first step on the ladder if you want to be a translator or a pharmacist.

All your school subjects are important and most of them will be GCSEs, however there are now other qualifications you may encounter that are also important in preparing and supporting you in further study and the world of work, and these include Key Skills.

What you learn

If you think about the days when you first went to school, you did not study Biology or History. You may well have learned about plants or the Vikings but this was all part of a more general approach to learning, which concentrated very much on getting you to read and understand, and also to use number confidently in things like adding up and knowing your tables.

You also learned to play during your first years at school and within play there are some important lessons. You have to take notice of what others say, you have to share toys and you have to work out how to do things, often in a group.

If you think about the skills you learned during those first few years at school you can see how they prepared you for all the learning you have done since. The same skills have also influenced how you behave with people and how you work with other people in a group situation.

The Key Skills

The Key Skills curriculum 'pulls out' just these sorts of general or transferable skills from the school work you are doing for your GCSEs and from all the other things you do at school, at home or in any paid employment you might have.

> It can be argued that subject knowledge can become out of date. Key Skills do not date because they can be transferred across a range of educational levels and a variety of settings. Employers, colleges and universities have recognised that these are the skills to equip you for life.

If you were to ask your parents or grandparents what they learned at school, you would discover that it was organised in a very different way. Often there were girls' and boys' subjects. What you learned depended on whether you passed the 11-plus exam and went to a Grammar School or a Secondary Modern School. Many children who went to Secondary Modern Schools learned subjects with a more practical bias, such as typing, office work and technical skills, while the children who 'passed' the 11-plus studied for their 'O' Levels and looked to go to university.

Since the introduction of comprehensive education there have been more opportunities for everyone to gain qualifications and develop their skills throughout their lives. In the past it was often difficult for people to change jobs/careers because they were only trained for one role. Opportunity does not stop at 11 or 16. Key Skills are designed to help you make the very most of yourself and to take every opportunity to develop yourself so that you **can** tackle your future schooling and work with confidence.

The Key Skills that you concentrate on over the next couple of years will probably be:

> **Communication (C)**
>
> **Application of Number (N)**
>
> **Information Technology (IT)**

If you achieve these three Key Skills, at whatever level, you will be awarded the **Key Skills Qualification**. Each Key Skill can also be achieved as a separate unit.

But these are not the only Key Skills. The 'wider' Key Skills are also important and you should not forget them, even if your school does not expect you to gain a qualification in them. They are:

> **Working With Others (WO)**
>
> **Problem Solving (PS)**
>
> **Improving Own Learning and Performance (LP)**

It would be useful for you to have a look at the Key Skills Specification for the wider Key Skills and see how your skills in these areas match the specifications. These three wider Key Skills contain things that may seem to have little to do with academic performance and getting exams. They are to do with how you relate to other people, how you plan your work and learning and how you deal with situations where you may be confronted with choices and alternatives. These are the very skills that employers value and that allow you to become more independent in your learning.

You could ask your teachers if they have copies of the wider Key Skills specifications or you can find them on the website of the Qualifications and Curriculum Authority (QCA): www.qca.org.uk.

Key Skills Level 2

> **This book will help you identify your existing strengths and weaknesses and develop your skills to achieve your Key Skills at Level 2.**

Key Skills have five levels and most schools and colleges will be working with students to achieve the Key Skills at Levels 1, 2 or 3. You can gain each of your Key Skills at a different level; they do not all have to be the same. So, for example, if you feel more confident with IT than with Application of Number, you could achieve a higher level in your Key Skills IT.

You must always work at a level that you feel comfortable with and then develop these existing skills further. You will not be able to produce evidence at the level required unless you are truly capable of working at that level. Key Skills are designed so that each level builds on the level below so you can see how your skills will develop and progress.

Do not make the mistake of thinking that Key Skills are not for you because you are aiming to go to university. Universities value Key Skills and many admissions tutors will take them into consideration when making offers of places. Key Skills at Level 3 and above also carry UCAS points.

If you think about it, very few university graduates actually use their degree subjects in their work. There are relatively few jobs for geographers, historians and mathematicians. So what do they do? Employers value the **skills** gained by graduates as well as the subject knowledge. At university these people have proved that they can organise their time, they can research information, they can synthesise and present information, they can work with other people and they can solve problems. This is what Key Skills are about.

REMEMBER...

This book will help you to help yourself in recognising and improving your Key Skills. Your teachers at school/college will also be able to offer you guidance and support to achieve the Key Skills Qualification.

All Key Skills have two elements:

PART A	What you need to know
PART B	What you need to do

If you haven't seen a Key Skills Specification before, have a look at the example in Appendix A. All specifications are laid out in the same way, for Level 1 through to Level 5.

Part A – What you need to know – is really the syllabus for that Key Skill, in this instance Application of Number Level 2. It is the list of the topics/skills that you will need to understand and demonstrate in order to pass the Key Skills **end test**.

At Levels 1 and 2, the end test is one hour long and consists of 40 multiple-choice questions, which will cover a selection of the skills outlined in Part A. You will not know what will be tested so you have to be confident across the whole range of Part A. Chapter 6 will give you more guidance on the end test.

At Level 2 in Application of Number there are three main areas that you will have to develop in order to be successful. These are:

INTERPRET INFORMATION

CARRY OUT CALCULATIONS

INTERPRET RESULTS AND PRESENT FINDINGS

You will also be required to produce a **portfolio of evidence** for Part B. The portfolio is explained further in Chapters 3 and 5.

If you look at the Specification in the Appendices, you will see that it is written as a set of standards that you must achieve and is broken down into detailed statements telling you what you need to know or do.

Key Skills are like any other qualification: you need to develop and practise in order to achieve a good result. The practice takes place in all the other activities you do in school and at home and your teachers can help by giving you feedback on your skills as well as your subject knowledge.

On the next page you will find some statements about Application of Number skills. Have a go at filling in the grid and identify where you think your strengths and weaknesses lie. Be honest with yourself – that is the only way you will start to improve and obtain the support you need.

Use the grid to assess whether you feel you are strong or weak in a particular skill. Put ticks in the appropriate boxes.

Can you do the following things?

Application of Number skill	Always	Sometimes	Never	SCORE
Obtain the information required				
Read and understand graphs, tables, charts and diagrams				
Understand negative numbers				
Estimate				
Read scales on equipment				
Make accurate observations/counts				
Select appropriate methods for gaining information				
Show how you carried out calculations				
Carry out multiple-stage calculations				
Convert between fractions, decimals and percentages				
Convert between systems, e.g. pounds to kilograms, Fahrenheit to centigrade				
Calculate areas and volumes				
Read off dimensions from scale drawings				
Use proportion and ratios				
Compare sets of data (20+ items)				
Understand the use of range in describing data				
Understand and use given formulae				
Check methods and calculations to identify and correct errors				
Present findings clearly and effectively				
Construct and use graphs, charts and diagrams				
Highlight the main points of your findings				
Describe your methods				
Explain how your results meet the purpose of your work				

Now score yourself.

Give yourself 2 for 'Always', 1 for ' Sometimes' and 0 for 'Never'.

There are 23 skill areas listed and the maximum score is 46. What did you score?

46	It may be that you are over-confident as such perfection is rare! When you look further into the Key Skills specifications you will see what the standards require of you and you may want to reconsider your answers.
25 or more	This would be a realistic assessment. You have lots of strengths on which you can build but you also recognise that you have some weaknesses. For example, you may never have had to describe your methods and explain how your results meet the purpose of your work. These are skills that you will gain as part of your Key Skills development.
Below 25	Are you being over-critical of your ability? Don't forget that at this stage you are working towards your Level 2 Key Skills in Application of Number. Don't punish yourself for not being perfect. If you feel that your skills with the four rules of number may let you down, don't ignore them. These rarely improve without some extra help and support and you will not be allowed to use a calculator in the end test. Get help now!

On the following pages you will find a description of the main points to remember when developing your Application of Number skills.

Interpreting information from different sources

Sources that you might use for Application of Number include statistical information in tables; the results of questionnaires; observations you have recorded yourself; graphs, charts and tables. Depending on your task, you will have to think widely when gathering the best evidence to produce results.

- Are you comfortable searching for a wide range of both IT and non-IT sources?

- Do you bookmark useful Internet sites that offer statistical information?

- Do you know where to find statistical information in the libraries that you use?

Read and understand	<ul><li>It is important that you not only find information, but that you understand what you have found and its significance.</li><li>At this level you need to understand what you are doing and not just follow instructions from your teacher</li></ul>
Estimate	<ul><li>Key Skills put great emphasis on checking your results. If you cannot estimate you will never know if your answer is accurate or not. This is particularly important as you are not allowed a calculator in the end test.</li><li>Estimating helps you gauge the magnitude of an answer: should it be 1000 or 10 000? By rounding and estimating you should be able to predict an approximate answer to check your work against.</li></ul>
Accurate observations	<ul><li>You will be required to record what you observe and to do it accurately. For example you could be doing a survey of traffic. How will you do this?</li></ul>
Grouping data	<ul><li>You will need to understand when and how to group data, e.g. ages 0–5 years, 6–10 years, 11–15 years etc.</li><li>This can be crucial when presenting data visually, in charts or graphs.</li></ul>

Opportunities for interpreting information

Science subjects usually give plenty of opportunities to collect and interpret data and information. Geography can also be a good source of information.

You will not find many opportunities for collecting numerical information in Humanities and Arts subjects. Do not waste your time looking for it; go for something more obvious and the evidence will be easier to develop. Ask your teacher's advice.

Carrying out calculations

Once you have collected information/data, you have to do something with it. In Application of Number there are some clear guidelines on 'what' it is you have to do. Some of these techniques are reviewed after this section.

Looking at the range of techniques required, are you confident in all of these without the aid of a calculator?

Multi-stage calculations	• Can you perform calculations that have more than one stage? For example: Stage 1 – 2 airfares at £167.00; Stage 2 – paid for in pesetas at 261 pesetas to the pound. 2 × £167 = £334, £334 × 261 = **87 174 pta**.
Percentages, fractions and decimals	• Converting between these three categories should be easy for you when using simple examples such as $\frac{1}{2}$, $\frac{1}{4}$, $\frac{1}{3}$ etc. • You should know how to work out the ones you do not know by heart.
Convert measurements between systems	• You should be able to read from a scale showing Fahrenheit to centigrade or pounds to kilograms. • Given the formula can you work between two systems?
Area and volume	• Can you work out the area and the volume of straightforward shapes? • Do you always remember to express your answer in m^2 for area and m^3 for volume?
Scale drawings	• Scale drawings are a good example of where estimation can come in useful. Is the measurement you have obtained from reading the scale drawing realistic? Estimating is a good way of checking. • Make sure you are expressing your answer in the correct units. Is it m or cm?
Ratios and proportion	• Ratios and proportion have important applications in 'real life' and you should make sure that you understand what they represent. • They are commonly used in cooking (half fat to flour), manufacturing (4 kg of powder to 10,000 litres of water) and in medicine (5 cc per 1 kg body weight).
Compare sets of data	• Can you use mean, median and mode to compare sets of data? • Do you know the best 'average' to use to describe your data in a particular situation?

Opportunities for carrying out calculations

There will be many opportunities for you to practise calculations within your Maths GCSE. However, this will **not** usually be appropriate for your Application of Number evidence. This is because you are only practising the techniques and not applying them to a substantial activity or a 'real life' situation.

Do not worry about this because it is really important that you do develop the techniques and skills **before** you try to apply them.

Interpreting results and presenting your findings

Interpreting and presenting your findings is as important in Application of Number as it is in the Communication and Information Technology Key Skills. There is no point in doing the work if you cannot communicate what you have done to other people. For this reason you have to be clear about the purpose of the work you are undertaking. How are you required to report your findings? Who will be the 'audience'? By answering these questions you should be able to identify the best way to present your findings.

Graphs, charts and diagrams	• These are all ways to give your results more visual impact and make it easier for your audience to understand your findings. Do you know which would be appropriate for your needs?
Highlight the main points of your findings	• If you wanted to highlight your main points you might produce a report that listed the main points, supported by your calculations, as an appendix.
Describe your methods	• Key Skills specifications always encourage you to say how and why you tackled a task or problem in the way you did. • As you progress through Key Skills levels you will be required to reflect on what you did and how you could improve next time. It is not a bad idea to start thinking about this, even at this level.
Explain how your results meet your purpose	• Usually the work that you have undertaken will have been in an attempt to answer a question: 'Can something be done?' or 'How much will something cost?' etc. • If you come up with a sensible answer that satisfies the question then you will usually have met your purpose.

Opportunities for interpreting results and presenting findings

Application of Number requires more from you than a couple of pages of calculations. You must 'explain' how you went about your task, what you found out and how you chose to present your findings. Application of Number is as much concerned with the 'process' of your activity as it is with the 'end result'.

The skills you use here will be drawn from Communication, IT and many other areas of your curriculum.

Some reminders...

It is not the purpose of this book to take you through a course in maths. On the following pages, however, you will find reminders of some of the techniques you should know by heart and will need to master in order to be successful in your end test – where you will be on your own…without a calculator!

Estimation

We use estimates all the time in everyday life. When buying food we round up or down because you cannot buy $\frac{1}{4}$ of a lettuce or $\frac{1}{2}$ an egg. We meet people when we finish school at **about** 3.30pm. Giving directions, we might say that the bus stop is **about** 100 m down the road. In many things we do, we don't require a great level of accuracy. If you told someone that the bus stop was 103.5 m down the road they might think you were mad!

> **Many estimates are to do with money. In this case you should always work to 2 decimal places.**

Estimation requires the skill of rounding up or down. To practise, complete the following table:

Number	d.p.	Answer
3.457	1	
0.764	2	
0.765	2	
8.2717	3	
8.2717	2	
0.086	1	
167.154	2	
167.154	1	
7.991	1	
7.996	2	

Ratios and proportion

If two trains are travelling at speeds of 120 miles per hour (mph) and 80 miles per hour (mph) their speeds are in the ratio of 120 : 80. It is usual to cancel down ratios to their lowest form.

So   120 : 80
is the same as   12 : 8
and   3 : 2

The trains' speeds are in a ratio of 3 : 2.

Express the following ratios in their lowest terms.

1   6 : 12

2   5 : 25

3   8 : 40

4   18 : 21

5   88 : 132

6   Fred makes nettle wine by using 3 kg white sugar to 12 kg of nettles. If he has 12 kg of sugar, how many kg of nettles does he need?

Measurement

Below are some of the most common units of measurement we use.

Imperial units

Length

12 inches	=	1 foot
3 feet	=	1 yard
1760 yards	=	1 mile

Weight

| 16 ounces | = | 1 pound |
| 14 pounds | = | 1 stone |

Capacity

| 20 fluid ounces | = | 1 pint |
| 8 pints | = | 1 gallon |

Metric units

Length

10 millimetres	=	1 centimetre
100 centimetres	=	1 metre
1000 metres	=	1 kilometre

Weight

1000 grams	=	1 kilogram
1000 kilograms	=	1 tonne

Capacity

1000 millilitres	=	1 litre

Approximate conversions for everyday use

Length

1 inch	=	2.5 cm
1 metre	=	39 inches or 1.09 yards
1 kilometre	=	$\frac{5}{8}$ of a mile

Weight

1 kilogram	=	2.2 lbs

Try these.

1 Change 8 inches to centimetres.

2 Change 56 km to miles.

3 Convert 132 lb to kilograms.

Fractions

The number on the top is called the   NUMERATOR

The number on the bottom is called the   DENOMINATOR

When the numerator and the denominator of a fraction are multiplied or divided by the same number, the value of the fraction remains the same.

Example: $\frac{1}{6}$ is the same as $\frac{2}{12}, \frac{3}{18}, \frac{4}{24}, \frac{5}{30}, \frac{6}{36} \ldots \frac{20}{120}$ etc.

$$\frac{1}{6} \begin{smallmatrix} \times 2 \\ \times 2 \end{smallmatrix} \rightarrow \frac{2}{12}$$

$$\frac{1}{6} \begin{smallmatrix} \times 3 \\ \times 3 \end{smallmatrix} \rightarrow \frac{3}{18}$$

To add or subtract fractions with the same denominators we can simply add or subtract the numerators.

Example: $\frac{4}{5} - \frac{2}{5} = \frac{2}{5}$ or $\frac{1}{5} + \frac{4}{5} = 1$

If the fraction has different denominators we have to change the denominators so that they are the same.

Example: $\frac{1}{6} + \frac{3}{4}$ must become $\frac{2}{12} + \frac{9}{12} = \frac{11}{12}$

(12 is the lowest common multiple of 6 and 4)

Now try these.

1   $\frac{3}{7} + \frac{3}{14} =$

2   $\frac{1}{2} + \frac{1}{5} =$

3   $\frac{1}{6} + \frac{5}{12} =$

4   $\frac{1}{2} + \frac{1}{5} + \frac{3}{10} =$

Multiplying and dividing fractions

When multiplying fractions the answer will always be smaller.

In order to multiply fractions you multiply the numerator by the numerator and the denominator by the denominator.

Example: $\frac{4}{5} \times \frac{2}{3} = \frac{8}{15}$

If you can, try cancelling before or after you do the sum. In this instance you cannot cancel.

Now try these.

5   $\frac{1}{4} \times \frac{1}{4} =$

6   $\frac{3}{4} \times \frac{1}{2} =$

7   $\frac{7}{14} \times \frac{3}{21} =$

8   $\frac{5}{6} \times \frac{2}{3} =$

9   $\frac{1}{2} \times 6 =$

10 $\frac{2}{5} \times 10 =$

To divide by fractions, remember to 'turn the number you are dividing by upside down, then multiply'.

Example: $\frac{1}{2} \div \frac{1}{4}$ is $\frac{1}{2} \times \frac{4}{1} = \frac{4}{2} = 2$

$\frac{1}{4} \div 2$ is $\frac{1}{4} \times \frac{1}{2} = \frac{1}{8}$

Now try these.

11 $\frac{3}{4} \div \frac{1}{12} =$

12 $\frac{1}{5} \div 2 =$

13 $\frac{4}{5} \div \frac{3}{8} =$

14 $\frac{7}{8} \div 5 =$

15 $\frac{2}{3} \div \frac{1}{6} =$

Percentages

'Per cent' means per hundred. 10 per cent is 10 out of a hundred and is written 10%.

Fractions and decimals can be written as percentages.

$\frac{1}{2}$ is the same as   0.5   which is the same as 50%

$\frac{1}{4}$ is the same as   0.25   which is the same as 25%

$\frac{1}{10}$ is the same as   0.10   which is the same as 10%

$\frac{1}{5}$ is the same as   0.20   which is the same as 20%

Changing fractions to percentages: multiply by 100 and then cancel down.

Example: $\frac{1}{4} \times 100 = \frac{1}{4} \times \frac{100}{1} = \frac{100}{4} = 25\%$

$\frac{2}{5} \times 100 = \frac{2}{5} \times \frac{100}{1} = \frac{200}{5} = 40\%$

Change these fractions to percentages.

1 $\frac{3}{4}$

2 $\frac{3}{5}$

3 $\frac{1}{8}$

Changing percentages to fractions: write the percentage as a fraction with the denominator 100, and cancel if possible.

Example: $20\% = \frac{20}{100} = \frac{1}{4}$

$50\% = \frac{50}{100} = \frac{1}{2}$

Try these.

4 70%

5 45%

6 35%

Mean, median, mode and range

Averages

An average is a single figure used to describe a set of data. It can be used to make comparisons and describe trends.

There are three commonly used averages:

> **Arithmetic mean**
>
> **Median**
>
> **Mode**

Arithmetic mean – The most commonly used average. To find the arithmetic mean, add all the values to be averaged together and divide by the number of items.

Example: Fred is 40, John is 35, Kate is 21 and Sanjit is 28. What is their average age?

(40 + 35 + 21 + 28) years ÷ 4 people = 31 years (average age)

The arithmetic mean can include a fraction or a decimal place; it is not always a whole number.

Calculate the following means.

1   3, 6, 9, 10, 12

2   161 cm, 165 cm, 167 cm, 179 cm

3   £5, £12, £17, £14

The median is the middle value when the values are arranged in order of size. Odd numbers of values will produce a single value in the middle. Even numbers have a median that is the **mean** of the middle two numbers.

So, to find the median of the following numbers: 22, 20, 11, 18, 30, 18, 15

write the data in order of size: 11, 15, 18, 18, 20, 22, 30

The middle value is 18, so the median is 18.

Now try these.

4   35, 64, 12, 18, 29, 56, 33, 40

5   3, 5, 8, 2, 8, 7, 11

6   19, 3, 17, 12, 15, 19, 19

The mode is the value that occurs most often. A set of data can have more than one mode: if two values appear the same number of times the data can be bi-modal.

Look at this weather data:

Weather	No. of days
Sunshine	18
Rain	15
Cloudy	13
High winds	18
Snow	8

The mode here is sunshine and high winds, because both occurred on 18 days. This data is bi-modal.

Find the mode for these data sets:

7 6, 2, 2, 4, 6, 3, 6, 4

8 4, 8, 8, 8, 3, 4, 5, 7, 1, 4, 6, 1, 7, 4, 3

9 a, b, b, c, d, a, a, c, d, d, c, c, a, a, a

All these averages are fairly easy to calculate and are used in different circumstances.

● The most commonly used is the arithmetic mean. Most people understand it but it can be distorted if the data has values that are very large or very small compared with the others. It can also give silly results like '2.4 children'!

● The median is useful to clarify a situation where there are extreme values in a set of data.

● The mode is useful in situations where you might need to know how many items were sold or used, for example in shops or offices.

Area, perimeter, volume and scale drawing

Area is the space taken up by a flat surface, like a carpet or tabletop.

It can also be a curved surface such as a coke can. (Imagine it opened out and laid flat).

Area is measured in square units:

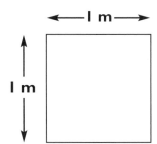

- This is a carpet (not to scale) with each side measuring 1 m in length.
- The area of this carpet is 1 square metre (1 m^2)
- If the sides were each 2 m, the area would be 4 m^2.

To find the area of a rectangle you multiply:

length x width

Perimeter – The perimeter is the total distance measured around the outer edges of a shape.

This work surface needs an edging glued around its perimeter. How much edging would you need to purchase?

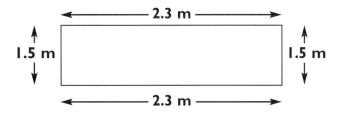

- To find the perimeter add: 1.5 + 1.5 + 2.3 + 2.3 = 7.6 m
- The perimeter of the work surface is 7.6 m.

Volume – To calculate the volume of a cube you use the formula:

> **length x width x height**

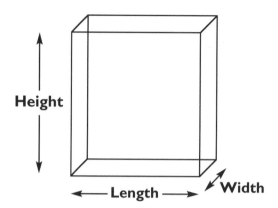

If the height is 12 cm, the length 10 cm and the width 5 cm, the volume of this cube would be:

12 x 10 x 5 = 600 cm³

Volume is always expressed in cubic units.

Scale diagrams represent real objects that we cannot draw on paper because they are too big. Because of this we have to 'scale' them down.

The scale can be:

● a comparison between two lengths

  I cm : 2 m (Every I cm on the diagram represents 2 m in real life.)

or

● a ratio

  I : 200 (All the measurements are $\frac{1}{200}$ of their size in the original.)

For example:

A diagram has a scale of I : 8. The length of a line on the drawing is 5 cm. What is its original length?

5 x 8 = 40 cm

Answers

Estimation

Number	d.p.	Answer
3.457	1	3.5
0.764	2	0.76
0.765	2	0.77
8.2717	3	8.272
8.2717	2	8.27
0.086	1	0.1
167.154	2	167.15
167.154	1	167.2
7.991	1	8.0
7.996	2	8.00

Ratios and proportion

1 6 : 12   (divide by 6)   =   1 : 2

2 5 : 25   (divide by 5)   =   1 : 5

3 8 : 40   (divide by 8)   =   1 : 5

4 18 : 21   (divide by 3)   =   6 : 7

5 88 : 132   (divide by 11)   =   8 : 12   (divide by 4)   =   2 : 3

6 The recipe for the wine is in a ratio of 3 sugar : 12 nettles. Fred has 12 kg of sugar. If you divide that by 3, you will find he has 4 times the quantity required for the recipe. He will, therefore, also need 4 times the quantity of nettles – 4 x 12 = 48 kg.

Measurement

1 8 x 2.5 = 20 cm

2 $\frac{56}{8}$ x 5 = 7 x 5 = 35 miles

3 $\frac{132}{2.2}$ = 60 kg

Fractions

1. $\frac{3}{7} + \frac{3}{14} =$ $\qquad$ $\frac{6}{14} + \frac{3}{14} = \frac{9}{14}$

2. $\frac{1}{2} + \frac{1}{5} =$ $\qquad$ $\frac{5}{10} + \frac{2}{10} = \frac{7}{10}$

3. $\frac{1}{6} + \frac{5}{12} =$ $\qquad$ $\frac{2}{12} + \frac{5}{12} = \frac{7}{12}$

4. $\frac{1}{2} + \frac{1}{5} + \frac{3}{10} =$ $\qquad$ $\frac{5}{10} + \frac{2}{10} + \frac{3}{10} = \frac{10}{10} = 1$

5. $\frac{1}{4} \times \frac{1}{4} =$ $\qquad$ $\frac{1}{16}$

6. $\frac{3}{4} \times \frac{1}{2} =$ $\qquad$ $\frac{3}{8}$

7. $\frac{7}{14} \times \frac{3}{21} =$ $\qquad$ $\frac{1}{2} \times \frac{1}{7} = \frac{1}{14}$

8. $\frac{5}{6} \times \frac{2}{3} =$ $\qquad$ $\frac{10}{18} = \frac{5}{9}$

9. $\frac{1}{2} \times 6 =$ $\qquad$ $\frac{6}{2} = 3$

10. $\frac{2}{5} \times 10 =$ $\qquad$ $\frac{20}{5} = 4$

11. $\frac{3}{4} \div \frac{1}{12} =$ $\qquad$ $\frac{3}{4} \times \frac{12}{1} = \frac{36}{4} = 9$

12. $\frac{1}{5} \div 2 =$ $\qquad$ $\frac{1}{5} \times \frac{1}{2} = \frac{1}{10}$

13. $\frac{4}{5} \div \frac{3}{8} =$ $\qquad$ $\frac{4}{5} \times \frac{8}{3} = \frac{32}{15} = 2\frac{2}{15}$

14. $\frac{7}{8} \div 5 =$ $\qquad$ $\frac{7}{8} \times \frac{1}{5} = \frac{7}{40}$

15. $\frac{2}{3} \div \frac{1}{6} =$ $\qquad$ $\frac{2}{3} \times \frac{6}{1} = \frac{12}{3} = 4$

Percentages

1. $\frac{3}{4} \times \frac{100}{1} =$ $\qquad$ $\frac{3}{1} \times \frac{25}{1} = 75\%$

2. $\frac{3}{5} \times \frac{100}{1} =$ $\qquad$ $\frac{3}{1} \times \frac{20}{1} = 60\%$

3. $\frac{1}{8} \times \frac{100}{1} =$ $\qquad$ $\frac{1}{2} \times \frac{25}{1} = \frac{25}{2} = 12.5\%$

4. $\frac{70}{100} =$ $\qquad$ $\frac{7}{10}$

5. $\frac{45}{100} =$ $\qquad$ $\frac{9}{20}$

6. $\frac{35}{100} =$ $\qquad$ $\frac{7}{20}$

Mean, median, mode and range

1. $\frac{40}{5} =$ $\qquad$ 8

2. $\frac{672}{4} =$ $\qquad$ 168 cm

3. $\frac{48}{4} =$ $\qquad$ £12

4. 12,18,29,33,35,40,56,64 = (33+35) ÷ 2 = 34

5. 2,3,5,7,8,8,11 = $\qquad$ 7

6. 3,12,15,17,19,19,19 = $\qquad$ 17

7. 6

8. 4

9. a

Up to now this book has concentrated on Part A of the Level 2 Key Skills Application of Number specification. Remember that Part A is the 'syllabus' containing all the skills you need to have in order to gain the Key Skills unit.

You need to have **all** of the skills listed in order to be successful at this level of Application of Number as the end test may ask you to demonstrate your ability to use any of these skills. Part B outlines the content required for your portfolio of evidence. This requires you to take your Application of Number skills and **apply** them to evidence from school, home or work in order to demonstrate your skills.

'Apply' is the important word here: Key Skills are about developing skills that can be used in many different ways and in many different settings.

> Application of Number Level 2 has three components for Part B. You must provide evidence for all three components.

The specification says what you must do and the bullet points add further detail to guide you when producing your evidence. These bullet points are also the things that you will be assessed on. If you have not covered all of these points you cannot achieve the Key Skills unit of Application of Number Level 2.

To remind yourself of the way that the specification is laid out, have another look at Appendix A.

The components

The following pages provide an explanation of what you must produce as evidence in your portfolio for each of the components for Application of Number Level 2.

You will not be ready to produce portfolio evidence until you have developed and practised the skills in Part A. However, this should not stop you thinking about your portfolio and trying to plan ahead to identify work you are doing that may provide evidence for your Application of Number Key Skill.

It is possible that you will find some evidence in your other qualifications **but** be very careful as work produced for other subjects may not fully conform to the Key Skills criteria. You may need to develop your work further to make sure you cover all the criteria.

Application of Number evidence may require you to take a piece of work you are already doing and develop it further to meet the wider requirements of the specification. Try not to end up with lots of little bits of evidence that do not form a substantial piece of work when put together. You will need to plan your work to provide the evidence you need and keep monitoring it as you produce your assignment.

N2.1 COMPONENT	EXPLANATION	CRITERIA	IDEAS FOR EVIDENCE
You must: Interpret information from **two** different sources, including material containing a graph.	The information you obtain should be **straightforward**: the sort of material or subject that you come across on a regular basis in your school, home or leisure activities. One of the sources must be a **graph**: line graphs, scatter graphs or cumulative frequency graphs are all examples of sources you could use.	Evidence must show you can: ● choose how to obtain the information needed to meet the purpose of your activity; ● obtain the relevant information; and ● select appropriate methods to get the results you need.	You must ensure that you have two sources of information and that one source contains a graph. Good sources will allow you to produce good evidence; it goes without saying that poor or limited sources will limit what you can produce. The key here is to plan carefully before you begin work on the calculations. Look at your sources – are they going to be sufficient to enable you to get the evidence? Think about N2.2 – do your sources lend themselves to formulae, scales, ratios and proportion etc.? In your evidence for this element you must clearly state the purpose of your activity and it should be a 'strong' statement, not something wishy-washy. 'Because it is a piece of X coursework' would not satisfy the assessor – the activity has to have a purpose beyond the fact that you have been told to do it. For example, your Geography coursework may require you to record different types of farming in a particular area and produce a report. That is the purpose; not that it is a piece of Geography coursework. Keep records of all your sources and of any information obtained, for example printouts, questionnaires produced and so on.

N2.2 COMPONENT	EXPLANATION	CRITERIA	IDEAS FOR EVIDENCE
You must: Carry out calculations to do with: **A** amounts and sizes **B** scales and proportion **C** handling statistics **D** using formulae	In your calculations you are required to show evidence of **multi-stage calculations**. These are calculations involving two steps or more. You should include a data set with at least **20 items**.	Evidence must show you can: ● carry out calculations, clearly showing your methods and levels of accuracy; and ● check your methods to identify and correct any errors, and make sure your results make sense.	Your evidence must clearly demonstrate that you have worked with all four categories of calculation. This is quite a tall order to achieve in any one piece of work. You may find that you have to produce another piece of work to cover the requirements. However, do try to get as much evidence as you can from one substantial activity. Can you develop that activity a bit further to meet all the requirements? If you do find yourself producing a second piece of work, it **must** again cover **all** the criteria, but activity 1 could cover, say, 'amounts and sizes' and 'scales and proportions', whilst activity 2 could cover 'handling statistics' and 'using formulae'. You must show clearly your methods and the levels of accuracy used. Most importantly you must show how you **checked** your work for errors. Checking your work for errors is a recurring theme with Key Skills and it is an important skill to develop. Don't lose marks because of silly errors. Do your results make sense? You should always have an idea (estimate) of your results. If you are nowhere near this estimate, have you made an error somewhere?

N2.3 COMPONENT	EXPLANATION	CRITERIA	IDEAS FOR EVIDENCE
You must: Interpret the results of your calculations and present your findings. You must use at least **one** graph, **one** chart and **one** diagram.	Some examples: **Graph:** line graphs, scatter graphs and cumulative frequency graphs **Chart:** pie charts, bar charts and histograms **Diagram:** maps, plans, scale drawings, network diagrams, flow charts and organisational charts	Evidence must show you can: ● select effective ways to present your findings; ● present your findings clearly and describe your methods; and ● explain how the results of your calculations meet the purpose of your activity.	When presenting your work and your findings, make sure you take every opportunity to display your skills in generating graphs, charts and diagrams to present your work in a visually attractive and informative way. Remember your presentation must be appropriate to your task. This can provide you with opportunities to demonstrate your IT skills, however, where possible, you should take the opportunity to explain why and how you have used IT to support your findings. You will not be penalised if you do not produce work using IT. All your methods should be clearly described and the results of your calculations clearly linked to the purpose of your task. If you imagine that the assessor looking at your work does not know you or what you have done, you can then produce a commentary to support your evidence. This is not **Maths**. It is applying number skills.

Suggestions for finding Key Skills Application of Number evidence

The following are some ideas of how your other subjects may provide Key Skills Application of Number evidence. Don't forget that **all** your work must be original and have been produced by you.

> At Level 2, your Application of Number evidence must come from a 'substantial activity'.

If you can get hold of the **specifications** for your GCSE subjects you will find that Key Skills opportunities are highlighted. This should give you a good idea of where you may be generating Key Skills evidence within the subject. If there are no copies easily available in school, go to the OCR website (www.ocr.org.uk) where you will find all of the specifications. It does not matter what awarding body your school uses – the Key Skills opportunities are the same. If you are uncertain about where to find this information, ask your teachers.

You will see from the table on the next pages that it can be difficult to find Application of Number evidence **directly** from your GCSE work. In fact, some of the GCSE specifications are not signposted at all for AON opportunities. Many of the awarding bodies acknowledge this and suggest that Application of Number evidence should be planned very carefully to ensure that it meets the specification.

If you are struggling to find Application of Number evidence from GCSEs, consider the wider curriculum – are you doing work in Citizenship or any other enrichment subjects that could be developed to produce number evidence?

REMEMBER...

> Application of Number is not Maths; it is taking your number skills and applying them to a problem you have to solve or a situation you find yourself in.

GCSE SUBJECT	N2.1	N2.2	N2.3	
ART AND DESIGN	X	X	X	Recording observations, analysing images, developing and exploring findings, reviewing and modifying work and then presenting a personal response are all skills in this subject that could lend themselves to AON. This subject is signposted for AON Level 2.
BIOLOGY	X	X	X	Within this specification there are signposts for all three components. The most likely areas for AON evidence are 'Organisms and Habitats' and 'Food Chains and Energy Flow'. Both are from the Ecology module.
BUSINESS STUDIES	X	X	X	The modules 'Business Communication and Marketing' and 'Business and Change' offer plenty of opportunities to evidence all three AON components.
CHEMISTRY	X	X	X	The module 'Rates of Reaction' is signposted for opportunities for evidence for all the components.
DESIGN AND TECHNOLOGY				This GCSE has no signposts for Application of Number Level 2, so be very careful if you want to develop evidence using work from this subject. Work involving planning workplace space or monitoring temperatures etc. may begin to give you a start in thinking about evidence that may meet the specification.
ENGLISH (existing specification – 2001)				This GCSE has no signposts for Application of Number Level 2, so be very careful if you want to develop evidence using work from this subject. Work on theatre attendance and costings, or looking at the health and safety requirements for putting on a production may give you evidence for Application of Number.

Subject			Description
GEOGRAPHY	X	X	In the module 'People and Places to Live' there are plenty of opportunities signposted to produce Application of Number evidence.
HISTORY			This GCSE has no signposts for Application of Number Level 2, so be very careful if you want to develop evidence using work from this subject. It would be easy to produce evidence that demonstrated your handling of statistics but the other criteria would be hard to develop.
ICT	X	X	Opportunities for linking Application of Number and IT should be quite straightforward. If you are doing the two Key Skills, it may be possible to use much of your evidence for both. This will require careful planning but would save you time in the long run. Do not forget that the evidence would have to fully meet the specifications for both Key Skills.
MATHS			It may surprise you to find that the Maths specification contains very little signposting for the Application of Number Key Skill. This should indicate that this is not a good GCSE from which to develop your number evidence. It may be easier to think more broadly when trying to produce your number work and apply your number skills to your other subjects.
PHYSICS	X	X	Physics has lots of signposting for Application of Number and the modules 'Force and Motion' and 'Radioactivity' both offer opportunities to develop your evidence.

If you are also doing your Key Skills Communication and IT, you should look carefully at the work you are producing for evidence and see if there is any 'cross-over'. If you are producing word-processed work for Application of Number and are doing research using the Internet, you may find that you can use some of your evidence for all three Key Skills – this is not cheating, it is allowed!

The following portfolio of evidence has been created for this book **for guidance only**. You should ensure that all the material you put in **your** portfolio is **original** and is **your own work**.

> This Unit Summary Sheet shows where the portfolio evidence can be found and that the portfolio is complete.

Newtown High School

Key Skills

①

> Don't forget to number the pages in your portfolio to make your evidence easy to find.

APPLICATION OF NUMBER LEVEL 2

CARRY THROUGH A SUBSTANTIAL ACTIVITY THAT INCLUDES STRAIGHTFORWARD TASKS FOR N2.1, N2.2 AND N2.3

COMPONENT		REFERENCE(S)
N2.1 Interpret information from **two** different sources, including material containing a graph.	Graph source Other source	A graph on air/water temperature was used in making calculations. Jenny also uses the graphs she creates as sources for her recommendations. A table of mean air temperatures was used as well as a scale drawing of the pool. (Page 3 and Page 5)
N2.2 Carry out calculations to do with: ● amounts and sizes ● scales and proportion ● handling statistics ● using formulae	Amounts and sizes Scales and proportion Handling statistics Using formulae	Calculations to obtain the area of the pool and proportions of chemicals in the pool. (Page 5) Calculations of wages and other costs of running the pool. (Pages 6 and 7) The questionnaire demonstrates the handling of statistical information. (Page 9) Formulae are used in area and volume work and within the spreadsheets. (Page 6)
N2.3 Interpret the results of your calculations and present your findings. You must use at least **one** graph, **one** chart and **one** diagram.	Graph Chart Diagram	The final report contains a graph, a chart and a diagram. (pages 12 - 14)

> You will sign the summary to confirm that this is your own work and the assessor (who may be your class teacher) will sign when they have assessed the portfolio.

ASSESSOR: Mandy Graney

DATE: 18 June 2001

CANDIDATE: Jenny Swift

DATE: 18 June 2001

This sheet records the assessment decision made on your work for Components N2.1, N2.2 and N2.3.

Newtown High School
Key Skills

These can be your comments or your assessor's comments on how you met the criteria.

CANDIDATE: Jenny Swift

PURPOSE OF TASK: To report to St Bridget's School governors on the costs of opening their swimming pool in July and August

N2.1 Interpret information from **two** different sources, including material containing a graph.	Graph source	Y p. 3	Other source	Y p. 3
N2.2 Carry out calculations to do with:	Amounts and sizes Scales and proportion	Y p. 5 Y p. 6	Handling statistics Using formulae	Y p. 9 Y p. 6
N2.3 Interpret the results of your calculations and present your findings. You must use at least **one** graph, **one** chart and **one** diagram.	Graph Chart Diagram	Y p. 13 Y p. 12 Y p. 12		

ASSESSMENT CRITERIA	HOW ASSESSMENT CRITERIA WERE MET
Choose how to obtain the information needed to meet the purpose of your activity.	Jenny describes clearly what she needs to do to complete the tasks. She was clear on the information she required and discussed this with me.
Obtain the relevant information.	Jenny was able to obtain the source data she required from people that she knew.
Select appropriate methods to get the results you need.	The evidence includes a list of tasks that she identified as necessary in carrying out this project. (Page 4)
Carry out calculations, clearly showing your methods and levels of accuracy.	Calculations throughout were done manually and then checked by calculator. Jenny chose to work to an accuracy of 2 d.p. which, in this instance, was appropriate for the task.
Check your methods to identify and correct any errors, and make sure your results make sense.	I questioned Jenny on her work in progress and was pleased that she was checking that her results made sense. She had to put all her findings into a 'real life' practical setting and realise that any major errors may have financial implications for the school.
Select effective ways to present your findings.	A report was an appropriate way to show her findings. The governors do not need to know all the calculations.
Present your findings clearly and describe your methods.	The use of a chart, a graph and a diagram allowed Jenny to present her findings in a clear manner and make the results easy to understand. Throughout the portfolio Jenny explains 'what' she is doing and 'why'.
Explain how the results of your calculations meet the purpose of your activity.	The calculations meet the purpose of the activity because the results of the calculations allow Jenny to produce a report to answer the question posed by the task.

ASSESSOR: **M. Graney**

DATE: **18 June 2001**

CANDIDATE: Jenny Swift

DATE: 18 June 2001

N2.1 Sources

Jenny Swift

Swimming pool plan.

Scale 1 : 250

Heating the pool.

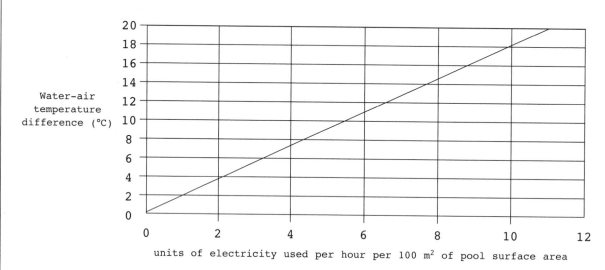

Month	J	F	M	A	M	J	J	A	S	O	N	D
Mean air temp °C	5	6	8	11	12	14	14	17	14	11	7	5

Key Skills Application of Number – Level 2
PORTFOLIO EVIDENCE

Jenny Swift

10C

TASK:

The task I chose to do for my evidence is to do with my mum being a governor at the local school for disabled children.

They have a really great outdoor swimming pool that does not get used in the summer when the school is closed. When my mum went to a governors' meeting last month, someone said 'Why don't we open the pool over the summer and charge people to use it?' Mum said there was lots of argument, basically because no one knew if it would be a sensible thing to do, because no one had worked out the costs.

I thought that I would work out the costs for the school and present my findings in a report to the governors. Then they will have something to base their decision on.

The pool would be:

1. Open for 8 weeks, Tuesday – Sunday, 10am – 4pm and closed an hour for lunch.

2. The pool must be kept at 20° centigrade.

3. The pool must have the correct chemicals for hygiene.

4. A pool attendant must be employed.

Things I need to do:

1. Work out the surface area of the pool.

2. Get some information about heat loss and electricity prices.

3. Work out the volume of the pool and calculate the quantity and cost of the chemicals needed.

4. Find out how much the attendant would be paid and work out the cost of employing him/her on an hourly basis.

5. Find out if people would use the pool.

I will work to two decimal places for all my calculations and all my calculations will be checked with my calculator.

The area of the pool

To find this out I measured the plan I got from the school.

It measured 7.2 cm by 10 cm. The scale was 1 : 250, therefore the real pool measures

7.2 x 250 = 1800 cm, 1800 ÷ 100 = 18 m

10 x 250 = 2500 cm, 2500 ÷ 100 = 25 m

18 m x 25 m = 450 m^2

> Amounts and sizes

> Multi-stage calculations

On to this I have to add the circular bit at the end.

To do this I measured the diameter of the circle, which was 3 cm. I divided this by 2 to get the radius and then x 250 to get its real size. This gave me 3.75 m.

I used the equation πr^2 to get the area of the circle and then divided this by 2 as it is a half circle.

> Use of formulae

3142 x (3.75)^2 = 44.18

44.18 ÷ 2 = 22.09 m^2

> Amounts and sizes

The total AREA of the pool = 22.09 + 450 = 472.09 m^2

Electricity prices

I asked the school Bursar about the cost of electricity to heat the pool and she told me it costs 6.8p a unit.

Outside temperatures

I went on the Met Office website and found a list of mean air temperatures for last year. I think that these will be accurate enough for me to get an estimate of costs.

Heat loss

At night a cover is put on the pool. This helps prevent heat loss.

I went to the local garden centre and asked if they had any information about pools and heating. I got a copy of the chart that they use when estimating for customers. It shows how much electricity it takes to keep a pool at a constant temperature.

With this information I can now work out electricity costs.

In July the mean air temperature is 14 degrees and in August it is 17 degrees. I am going to take each month as a 25-day period to make things easier.

In July the temperature in the pool has to be raised 6° to make it 20°. (20 − 14)

Reading from the graph this means that it takes 3.5 units of electricity per hour per 100 m² of pool surface.

25 days x 6 hours x 3.5 units of electricity x 4.72 (area of pool/100 m²) x 6.8(p) = 16850.4

Cost of heating pool in July = £168.50

Cost of heating for one day = £168.50 ÷ 25 = £6.74

In August the temperature in the pool has to be raised 3° to make it 20°. (20 − 17)

Reading from the graph this means that it takes 2 units of electricity per hour per 100 m² of pool surface.

25 days x 6 hours x 2 units of electricity x 4.72 (area of pool/100 m²) x 6.8(p) = 9628.8

Cost of heating pool in August = £96.29

Cost of heating pool for one day = £96.29 ÷ 25 = £3.86

Chemical treatment

Every 10 days the pool has to be cleaned with chemicals. This would not normally be done during the holiday period.

I spoke to the caretaker who told me that he has to use 100 grams of cleaning powder to every 10 m³ of the pool volume. The cleaning powder is in 20 kilo drums and costs £38.50 per drum.

I know the area of the pool surface and I am going to take an average depth of the pool as 1.8 metres.

Scales and proportion

Volume = l x w x h

Use of formulae

(l x w) 472.09 x 1.8 = 849.76 m³

Volume of the pool is 849.76 m³

To find the quantity of powder needed

849.76 ÷ 10 = 84.97 x 100 grams = 8497.6 grams ÷ 1000 = 8.50 kilos

20 kilos of cleaning powder costs £38.50, so 1 kilo costs = 38.5 ÷ 20 = 1.93

8.50 kilos x £1.93 = £16.41 ← Multi-stage calculations

Every time the pool is cleaned it costs £16.41.

The pool will be cleaned 4 times during the summer. In both July and August it will cost £32.82 to keep the pool clean.

Staffing

One of the students from my school is a qualified lifeguard and has said she would be interested in doing this job at the pool over the summer because she wants to make some money before going to university.

I looked in the local papers and found that the local authority pays pool attendants £4.20 an hour and time-and-a-third on Sundays. (4.20 x $1\frac{1}{3}$ = 5.60)

July

21 days x 5 hours x 4.20   = 441.00

4 days x 5 hours x 5.59   = 112.00

Total staffing costs = £553.00

August would be the same.

Usage of the pool

I realised that I have found out what it will cost to open the pool during the summer but I do not know how much money the pool is likely to earn during those months. Because it had never been open in the summer before I could not look at any figures.

I decided to do a questionnaire with my school friends and their families to see if they would use the pool.

The questionnaire is on the next page.

QUESTIONNAIRE ON ST BRIDGET'S POOL

St Bridget's School is considering opening its outdoor swimming pool over the months of July and August. I am doing a project to find out if there is any demand for this.

Please circle your answer(s):

Would you use St Bridget's Pool? **Yes   No**

If **'YES'** please answer the following questions:

Which days would you use the pool?	**T**	**W**	**TH**	**F**	**SA**	**SU**

How many times a week would you use the pool?	**1**	**2**	**3**	**4**	**5**	**6**

When would you use the pool?   **AM   PM**

What do you think is about the right entry price for:

Adults?	**£1**	**£1.50**	**£2**	**£2.50**

Children?	**50p**	**75p**	**£1**	**£1.50**

Thank you for your help.

Jenny Swift

10C

Newtown High School

I questioned 80 people and these are the results of my findings:

N = 80

Q.1

	YES	NO
Would you use St Bridget's Pool?	65 = 81%	15 = 19%

Q.2

	T	W	TH	F	SA	SU
Which days would you use the pool?	10	17	25	23	56	45

Mean daily usage: 176/6 = 29.33 or 30

Q.3

	1	2	3	4	5	6
How many times a week would you use the pool?	19	17	11	7	8	3

Total number of visits: 172

Median usage: between 3 and 4 times a week

Range: 5

Q.4

	AM	PM
When would you use the pool?	39 = 60%	26 = 40%

The **mode** for using the pool is AM.

Q.5

ADULT	£1	£1.50	£2	£2.50
What do you think is about the right entry price?	37	19	5	4
CHILD	50p	75p	£1	£1.50
What do you think is about the right entry price?	43	11	7	4

It is clear from the results that people are not prepared to pay much more than £1.50 per adult and 50p per child.

RESULTS:

In order to make sense of my findings I must go back to my original costs for running the pool in July and August:

July   £754.32

August   £682.11

My questionnaire only went to a small sample of friends but I need to know just how realistic it is to open the pool and I cannot assume that loads of people will come to use it.

Q.3 asked people how many visits they would make. I multiplied the number of visits by the number of people answering and got 172 visits over a 6 day opening.

172/6 = 29ish — I rounded this up to 30 visits a day.

I decided to assume that this represents 10 adults and 20 children and worked out some costs:

10 adults   per day at £1   = £10

20 children   per day at 50p   = £10

Income per day   = £20 x 25 days = £500

But

10 adults   per day at £1.50   = £15

20 children   per day at 75p   = £15

Income per day   = £30 x 25 days = £750

In order to break even over the summer period I think that the cost to enter the pool would have to be no less than £1.50 per adult and 75p per child. This is based on the attendance figures above.

I also decided to change my spreadsheet and see what happened if the hours of opening are reduced and if the pool only opened 5 days a week, i.e. closed on Tuesdays.

July

20 days x 6 hours x 3.5 units x 4.72 x 6.8p = £134.80

25 days x 6 hours x 3.5 units x 4.72 x 6.8p = £168.50

If the pool was closed on Tuesdays, which seems the least popular day, wages of 5 days x 5 hours x £4.20 would be saved = £105

NB: The pool has to be heated for 6 hours a day but it is closed at lunchtime, so it is only staffed for 5 hours.

A potential saving in July of £168.50 (25 days' electricity costs) — £134.80 (20 days' electricity costs) = £33.70

August

20 days x 6 hours x 2 units x 4.72 x 6.8p = £77.03

25 days x 6 hours x 2 units x 4.72 x 6.8p = £96.29

If the pool was closed on Tuesdays, which seems the least popular day, wages of 5 days x 5 hours x £4.20 would be saved = £105

A potential saving in August of £96.29 (25 days' electricity costs) — £77.03 (20 days' electricity costs) = £19.26

Report to the Governors of St Bridget's School

Subject: Pool opening July and August

I investigated the costs of opening the pool in July and August to see if a profit could be made for the school fund.

The costs of opening the pool are made up from the following items:

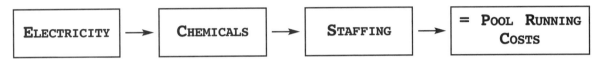

ELECTRICITY → CHEMICALS → STAFFING → = POOL RUNNING COSTS

Diagram

I used a range of sources to obtain this information and the results are as follows:

ITEM	July	Aug
Electricity	£168.50	£96.29
Staffing	£553.00	£553.00
Chemical Treatment	£32.82	£32.82
Total Costs	**£754.32**	**£682.11**

These costs show the pool running costs for each month if it is open 25 days a month for 5 hours a day, 10am — 4pm with an hour for lunch.

Chart

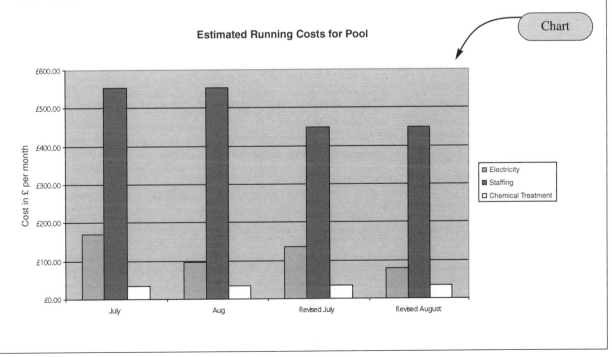

Estimated Running Costs for Pool

Report Page 2

It is clear from the chart that staffing is the biggest cost in opening the pool.

I had found out the costs of opening the pool but still did not know if anyone would want to use it. I designed a short questionnaire and used it with my friends and classmates. Out of 80 people questioned, 65 would use the pool. Some would use it more than once a week. However, they were not prepared to pay more than £1.50 per adult and 75p per child. I looked at the answer to how many would use the pool each day and decided it would be about 30. If I take this as 10 adults and 20 children, the monthly income over 25 days would be £750. However, not many people seemed to want to use the pool on Tuesdays and I did the calculations to find out how much the cost of running the pool could be reduced by closing on Tuesdays.

ITEM	July	Aug	Revised July	Revised August
Electricity	£168.50	£96.29	£134.80	£77.03
Staffing	£553.00	£553.00	£448.00	£448.00
Chemical Treatment	£32.82	£32.82	£32.82	£32.82
Total Costs	**£754.32**	**£682.11**	**£615.62**	**£557.85**

I have assumed that the income remains the same but that costs can be reduced by only opening for 20 days each month:

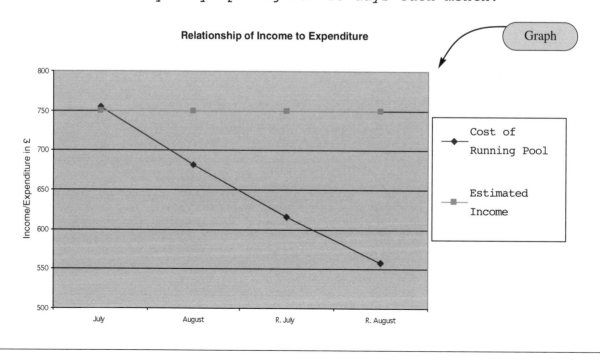

Relationship of Income to Expenditure

Graph

Report Page 3

RECOMMENDATIONS

- It is worthwhile opening the pool in July and August
- The pool should only be opened 20 days each month
- The pool should be open 10am — 4pm, closed for lunch 1 — 2pm
- A lifeguard should be employed at £4.20 per hour and time-and-a-third on Sunday
- The entry charge should be £1.50 for adults and 75p for children
- Some money should be spent on publicity to make sure as many people as possible know the pool is open
- The governors should investigate the opportunities to use the pool for birthday parties

Jenny Swift

May 2001

Sample test and commentary

The following is an example of an Application of Number Level 2 end test. It is a multiple-choice paper of 40 questions and the time allowed is one hour. Candidates are given a 'computer marked' sheet on which to record their answers.

There are, at the time of writing, up to five opportunities a year for candidates to sit the Level 2 end test. On each occasion the test will contain different questions but will be common to all of the awarding bodies that offer Key Skills awards. You will sit your end test on the date designated by QCA (Qualifications and Curriculum Authority) and the awarding bodies. There can be no exceptions – if you cannot sit your test on that day you will have to wait until the next test series, usually about eight weeks. Results are notified to your school about eight weeks after the tests. Your teachers will have more information on these dates.

It is hoped that, in the future, tests will be downloaded from the Internet and will be available on demand.

Now have a look over the following pages in this chapter and try to identify which questions you would have got right and which you would have got wrong. Read the comments on each question and think about Part A, the first bit of the Unit Specification.

The questions all require you to read quite quickly and extract the information required. This is where your reading and summarising skills come in. Make sure you read the questions carefully. Sometimes they seem very obvious but that is not always the case. You are being asked to read and answer questions about topics that you may never have come across before. This is where the **application** of your Application of Number skills comes in – you can use these skills whatever the topic. Do you think you know and understand enough to pass this end test or do your underpinning skills need more development?

REMEMBER...

> **Until you pass the end test you cannot achieve the Key Skill Unit.**

KEY SKILLS

APPLICATION OF NUMBER

Level 2

Question Paper

29 January 2001

WHAT YOU NEED

- This Question Paper
- An Answer Sheet
- A ruler marked in mm and cm

You may use a bilingual dictionary
Calculators are NOT permitted

Do NOT open this Question Paper until you are told to by the supervisor

THERE ARE 40 QUESTIONS IN THIS TEST
Total marks available: 40

Try to answer ALL the questions
TIME ALLOWED: 1 HOUR

INSTRUCTIONS

- Ensure that your personal details are entered correctly on the Answer Sheet
- Read each question carefully
- Follow the instructions on how to complete the Answer Sheet
- At the end of the test, hand the Question Paper, the Answer Sheet and all notes to the supervisor

---

REMEMBER: YOU HAVE 1 HOUR TO FINISH THE TEST

Questions 1 to 4 are about the sales at an ice-cream stall.

Liz runs an ice-cream stall. To check how popular each flavour is, she records the number of each flavour sold.

FLAVOUR OF ICE-CREAM	NUMBER SOLD
Strawberry	4
Mint Choc Chip	5
Raspberry	7
Chocolate	14
Banana	3
Toffee	6
Vanilla	8
Tutti Frutti	3

1   Which ice-cream flavour sold only two-thirds as many as toffee?

         A   Banana

         B   Strawberry

         C   Mint Choc Chip

         D   Tutti Frutti

2   What percentage of all the sales was the chocolate flavour?

         A   7%

         B   14%

         C   28%

         D   30%

3   Liz used 1 litre of vanilla ice-cream.

How much chocolate ice-cream did she use if all the ice-creams were the same size?

         A $\frac{4}{22}$ litre

         B $\frac{4}{7}$ litre

         C $1\frac{3}{4}$ litres

         D $2\frac{1}{2}$ litres

Application of Number Level 2: 29 January 2001

2

4   Additional data was recorded from a group of children who all had tutti frutti
     ice-cream. This made tutti frutti the unique mode for all the data.

     What is the minimum number of children in the group to give this statistic?

         A   3

         B   11

         C   12

         D   17

Please go on to the next page.

Some friends are planning a camping holiday in May.

5   The table shows information on the prices of some of the campsites available.

Campsite Information

Site	Price per night	Discounts
Happy Camper	£10 per tent	50% off third night
Rovers' Rest	£4 per tent plus £2 per person	–
Vibram Farm	£15 per tent	25% off all nights in May
Wood Nook	£2 per tent plus £4 per person	–

There are 4 people in the group and they are taking 2 tents for 3 nights in May.

They calculate that Rovers' Rest is the cheapest for them and Vibram Farm would be the most expensive.

How much would they save by going to Rovers' Rest rather than Vibram Farm?

     A   £6.50

     B   £8.50

     C   £19.50

     D   £25.50

6   There is a brilliant surfing beach 25 kilometres from Rovers' Rest but no one can remember its name.

One of the friends has a map with a scale of 2cm to 5km and he measures the distance from Rovers' Rest on the map to 4 local beaches.

Which one is the surfing beach?

A	Blackrock Sands	2cm
B	Gull Cove	5cm
C	St Peter's Bay	7cm
D	Whitesands	10cm

7   Their car uses 1 litre of petrol to travel 14.8 kilometres. The campsite is 88 kilometres away from their home town. They estimate how much fuel they will need for the trip there and back.

Which of these 4 attempts gives the closest estimate of the fuel required?

A $90 \div 15 = 6$ litres

B $90 \div 10 = 9$ litres

C $180 \div 15 = 12$ litres

D $180 \div 10 = 18$ litres

8   One of the items on their list of supplies is 6 yoghurts. The supermarket has several special offers.

Which would work out cheapest?

A   Original price 26p: buy one, get a second half-price

B   Original price 26p: buy two, get the third free

C   Original price 27p: one third off

D   Original price 28p: 25% off

Application of Number Level 2: 29 January 2001

5

Questions 9 and 10 are about sale labels in a clothes shop.

Kay has been given 4 labels to put on the sale rails at the clothes shop where she works.

1
> **Amazing**
> $\frac{1}{3}$
> Off!

Massive
> 20%
> Off!
2

3
> **Slashed**
> By
> 30%!

Half
> Original
> Price
4

9   Which label should she put on the trousers that are down from £24 to £16?

       A   Label 1

       B   Label 2

       C   Label 3

       D   Label 4

10   Which label should she put on the coats that are down from £50 to £35?

       A   Label 1

       B   Label 2

       C   Label 3

       D   Label 4

Application of Number Level 2: 29 January 2001

6

11   Which pie chart shows the results in this table?

Colour of car	Number of cars
Red	60
Blue	15
White	30
Black	15

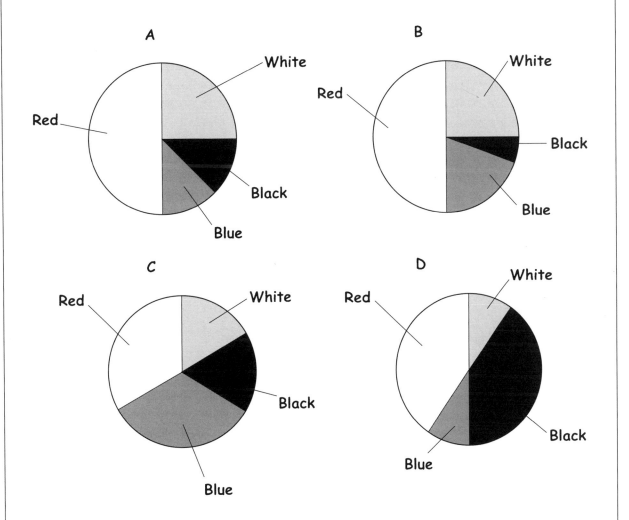

Questions 12 to 15 are about the balance sheet for a small business.

A business has a bank balance of £300 in January. The balance sheet for the first 8 months of the year is shown below, but some of the amounts are missing.

Balance Sheet

	Jan	Feb	Mar	Apr	May	Jun	Jul	Aug
Sales (£)	256	321	317	352			528	684
Expenses (£)	421	403	416		375	362	372	
Profit or Loss (£)	−165	−82		−49	3	35		331
Bank Balance (£)	135	53	−46	−95		−57		430

Profit or Loss = Sales – Expenses

12 What were the sales in June?

    A   £327

    B   £378

    C   £397

    D   £401

13 What were the expenses in April?

    A   £353

    B   £378

    C   £397

    D   £401

14 What was the profit or loss in March?

    A   −£99

    B   −£92

    C   £99

    D   £156

15 What was the bank balance in July?

    A   −£99

    B   −£92

    C   £99

    D   £156

Application of Number Level 2: 29 January 2001

8

16   An article in the local newspaper about the prices of new cars includes the following statement:

"Car prices rose steadily until January and then started to fall."

Which is the correct graph to match the statement?

A

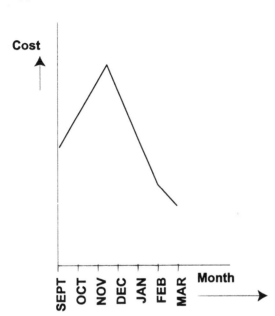

B

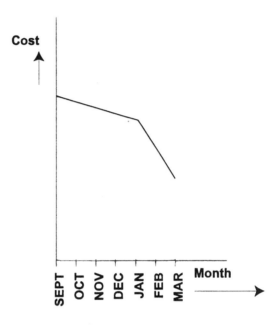

C

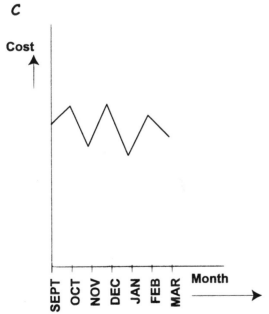

D

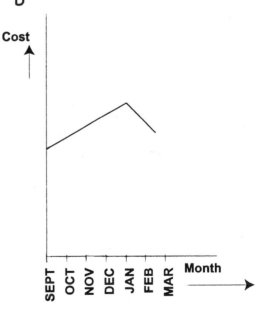

Application of Number Level 2: 29 January 2001

9

Questions 17 and 18 are about the construction of a sandpit for a children's nursery.

Two of the parents are making a round sandpit for the children.

It has a radius of 1.5 metres and a depth of 0.2 metres.

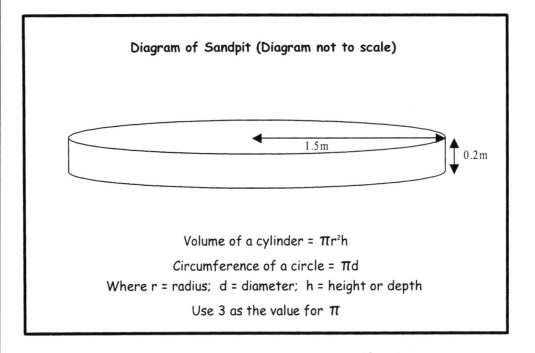

Diagram of Sandpit (Diagram not to scale)

Volume of a cylinder = $\pi r^2 h$

Circumference of a circle = πd

Where r = radius; d = diameter; h = height or depth

Use 3 as the value for π

17   What is the volume of sand needed to fill the sandpit?

     A $0.18m^3$

     B $1.35m^3$

     C $1.80m^3$

     D $6.75m^3$

18   Coloured warning tape will be put all the way round the top edge of the sandpit.

How much tape will be needed?

     A   4.5m

     B   6m

     C   6.75m

     D   9m

Application of Number Level 2: 29 January 2001

10

Questions 19 and 20 are about a trip to Greece.

George and Pat are going on holiday to Greece.

19 Pat exchanged £200 for 104 000 drachmas.

George exchanged £350 at the same exchange rate.

How many drachmas did George get?

    A   18 200

    B   59 428

    C   182 000

    D   673 076

20 Pat has a choice of 4 suitcases and wants to take the one that will hold the most.

Which case has the biggest volume?

    A   60cm x 45cm x 25cm

    B   60cm x 50cm x 20cm

    C   70cm x 50cm x 15cm

    D   80cm x 45cm x 15cm

Questions 21 and 22 are about the results of a typing test.

Four typists who are applying for a job are being assessed. Each has to type 10 items and the numbers of mistakes are counted.

Results of Assessment
Number of mistakes on each item of typing

Item	1	2	3	4	5	6	7	8	9	10
Alena	2	6	5	2	5	1	6	3	6	5
James	3	1	7	5	1	5	7	2	6	0
Mark	3	7	2	3	9	3	3	2	9	5
Stella	6	6	1	8	3	2	4	6	5	3

21   The number of mistakes for James' tenth item was incorrectly recorded as zero.

His mean score is 4.

What was the correct result for his tenth assessment?

        A   2

        B   3

        C   4

        D   5

22   The assessor wants to know which applicant is the most inconsistent.

Which measure would be the most appropriate to use?

        A   mode

        B   median

        C   range

        D   maximum value

Application of Number Level 2: 29 January 2001

12

Questions 23 and 24 are about 2 pie charts drawn from the results of a survey.

The survey was carried out as part of a catering course, to find out what 40 people ate in the canteen on 2 days of one week.

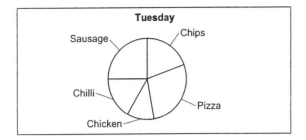

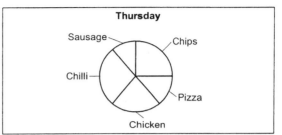

23   Which 2 items were more popular on Tuesday than on Thursday?

        A   Chicken and Chips

        B   Pizza and Chilli

        C   Pizza and Sausage

        D   Chicken and Chilli

24   The sector that represents Chips on Thursday is 90°.

    How many people does this represent?

        A   90

        B   40

        C   36

        D   10

25   Chris buys 4 CDs at £13.99 each. He gives the cashier £60.

    Which method would give Chris the closest estimate to let him check his change?

        A   60 - 13 × 4

        B   60 - 4 - 13

        C   60 - 4 + 14

        D   60 - 4 × 14

Application of Number Level 2: 29 January 2001

13

26   A carpet company has some floor plans.

Which floor plan represents an area of 109m ^{2} ?

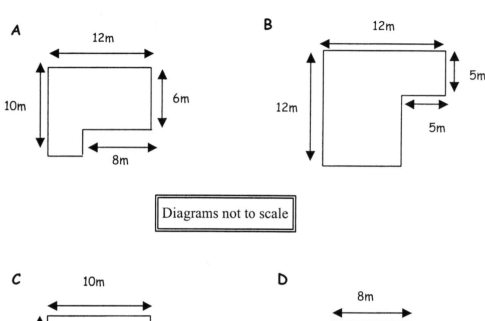

A

12m

10m   6m

8m

B

12m

12m   5m

5m

Diagrams not to scale

C

10m

10m   4m

3m

D

8m

12m   4m

10m

Questions 27 and 28 are about a recipe for making biscuits.

Jake is making 55 biscuits for the playgroup Christmas party.

He has a recipe for 20 biscuits, which requires:

> 150g margarine
> 150g sugar
> 1 egg
> 300g self-raising flour
> 50g ground almonds

27   How much flour will he need to make exactly 55 biscuits?

    A   413g

    B   825g

    C   900g

    D   1 650g

28   What is the ratio of ground almonds to sugar to self-raising flour in the recipe?

    A   3 : 6 : 1

    B   6 : 1 : 3

    C   1 : 3 : 6

    D   1 : 6 : 3

29   Sam has to carry out a survey to find out the proportion of students who travel to college by bus.

    Which group of people would it be most useful to interview?

    A   people at the town's bus station

    B   people at the nearest bus stop

    C   people entering the college

    D   people in the college's staff car park

Application of Number Level 2: 29 January 2001

15

30   In a competition to win a holiday you have to decide which of the following amounts of foreign money is worth the most:

         10 800 Danish kroner
         9 285 French francs
         2 610 000 Italian lire
         2 000 Swiss francs

The local newspaper gives the current exchange rates as:

         £1 = 12 Danish kroner
         £1 = 10 French francs
         £1 = 3 000 Italian lire
         £1 = 2.5 Swiss francs

Which of the amounts in the competition is worth the most in £s sterling?

     A   Danish kroner

     B   French francs

     C   Italian lire

     D   Swiss francs

31   Betty plans to hire a minibus for a 4-day scout camp. She estimates that she will do a total of 125 miles. The hire company charges £30 per day plus 15p per mile.

How much will the minibus cost for the trip?

     A   £121.87

     B   £138.75

     C   £180.00

     D   £245.00

32   A pop concert has an audience of 8 496 people. Two thirds of the people at the concert pay a £15 entrance fee while the remainder pay a reduced rate of £7.

What is the income from the concert to the nearest thousand pounds?

     A   £80 000

     B   £82 000

     C   £104 800

     D   £105 000

Application of Number Level 2: 29 January 2001

16

33   Caroline wants to know the weight of a chicken so that she can work out how long to cook it.

First she puts a dish on the scales and records the weight of the dish.

Then she weighs the dish with the chicken in it.

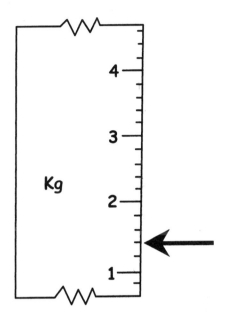 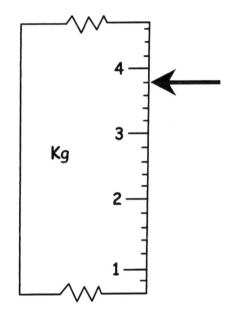

       DISH ONLY   **DISH AND CHICKEN**

How heavy is the chicken?

     A   2.2kg

     B   2.3kg

     C   2.4kg

     D   2.7kg

Application of Number Level 2: 29 January 2001

34 Bimla carried out a survey to find out the most popular pet.

Which way of showing the results would most likely be the easiest to understand?

A   frequency table

B   pictogram

C   scattergram

D   sectional bar chart

35 120 people are invited to the Christmas Party at work.

$\frac{1}{6}$ were not able to come because they were doing other things.

20% of those left did not want to come.

$\frac{1}{8}$ of those who said they would come had to cancel at the last minute.

How many people came to the party?

A   70

B   75

C   82

D   84

36 Ali needs an 18-inch zip to replace a broken one in a cushion. The shop only sells them in centimetres.

Which zip is the closest to the one Ali needs given that 1 inch is approximately equal to 2.5cm?

A   7cm

B   36cm

C   45cm

D   54cm

Application of Number Level 2: 29 January 2001

37 Maria is doing research into food storage temperatures for her catering course.
    She finds the following table in a book.

8°C	By law, perishable goods for public consumption must not be stored above this temperature.
5°C	By law, this is the highest temperature for very high risk food in a fridge.
3°C	Ideal temperature for a domestic refrigerator.
-6°C	One star rated freezer (*)
-12°C	Two star rated freezer (**)
-18°C	Three star rated deep freeze (***)

Her domestic refrigerator has a fault and is 4°C higher than the ideal temperature.

What is the difference in temperature between her domestic refrigerator and the three star rated deep freeze if the deep freeze is at the correct temperature?

    A   17°C

    B   19°C

    C   25°C

    D   27°C

38 An architect is making a scale model of a new house from a drawing.

    One of the dimensions on the drawing shows that the height of the real house is 12.5 metres.

    What scale does the architect need to work to, if the height of the model house has to be 2.5 centimetres?

    A   1 : 5

    B   1 : 50

    C   1 : 100

    D   1 : 500

Application of Number Level 2: 29 January 2001

Questions 39 and 40 are about decorating a bedroom.

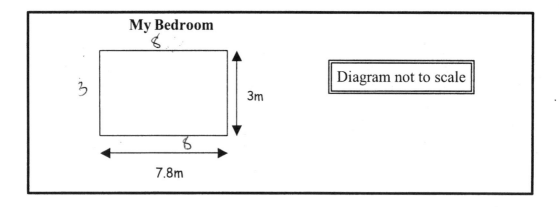

My Bedroom

3m

Diagram not to scale

7.8m

39   The border for the top of the walls costs £3.97 per metre.

Which estimate is most accurate for the total cost of the border?

A   (8 + 3) x 4 = £44

B   (8 + 3 + 8 + 3) = £22

C   (8 + 3) x 2 x 4 = £88

D   (8 x 3) x 4 = £96

40   3.2 litres of paint are needed to decorate the bedroom. (1 litre = 1 000cm^3).

The decorator mixes 3 paint colours together.

The amounts of paint are in the ratio:

15 parts of Honey Yellow to 12 parts of Aztec Orange to 5 parts of Ravishing Red.

How much Ravishing Red will she need?

A   500cm^3

B   720cm^3

C   1 067cm^3

D   1 200cm^3

END OF TEST

First published in 2001 © Qualifications and Curriculum Authority 2001

Reproduction, storage, adaptation or translation, in any form or by any means, of this publication is prohibited without prior written permission of the publisher, unless within the terms of licences issued by the Copyright Licensing Agency. Excerpts may be reproduced for the purpose of research, private study, criticism or review, or by educational institutions solely for educational purposes, without permission, provided full acknowledgement is given.

Printed in Great Britain

The Qualifications and Curriculum Authority is an exempt charity under Schedule 2 of the Charities Act 1993.

Qualifications and Curriculum Authority, 83 Piccadilly, London W1J 8QA   www.qca.org.uk

Answers and comments on the end test

Question	Answer	
1	B	Toffee sold 6, so the answer is $\frac{2}{3}$ of 6 = 4. Looking in the table, **strawberry** sold 4.
2	C	The total sold was 50 ice-creams. Chocolate sold 14, therefore 14 ÷ 50 = **28%**.
3	C	1 litre of vanilla made 8 ice-creams; each takes $\frac{1}{8}$ litre of ice-cream. Therefore 14 chocolate ice-creams would take $14 \times \frac{1}{8} = \frac{14}{8} = 1\frac{3}{4}$ **litres**.
4	C	Tutti frutti sales must be greater than chocolate sales of 14; the minimum number of additional sales must be **12**. 12 + 3 (existing sales) = 15. This would mean tutti frutti would be the unique mode for the data.
5	C	Rovers' Rest would cost: 2 x £4 for the tents, 4 x £2 for the people, all x 3 nights = £48 in total. Vibram Farm would cost: 2 x £15 for the tents x 3 nights, less 25% = £67.50. The group would save **£19.50** by going to Rovers' Rest.
6	D	To find out where the beach is on the map, divide 25 km by 5 km = 5, x 2 cm = 10 cm. You need to find a beach on the map that is 10 cm from Rovers' Rest. This is **Whitesands**.
7	C	There and back the journey is 2 x 88 km. Round this up to 2 x 90 = 180. Kilometres per litre is 14.8. Round this to 15. The estimate you require is **180 ÷ 15 = 12 litres** of fuel.
8	B	Price per yoghurt is a) 19.5p, b) 17.3p, c) 18p and d) 21p. The cheapest way to buy yoghurt is b) **buy two, get the third free**.
9	A	£24 less $\frac{1}{3}$ = £16, therefore **Label 1** shows $\frac{1}{3}$ off.
10	C	To find a 30% discount on £50 multiply by 70% = £35. **Label 3** is the correct one.
11	A	In order to find the proportions you need to add up all the cars. In total there are 120. Red with 60 cars = 50% of 120 and white with 30 cars = 25% of 120. Both A and B would fit this requirement so you then have to look at blue and black which have equal numbers of cars. Only **A** fits this pattern.
12	C	Sales – expenses = profit/loss so for June, sales – 362 = 35 or re-arranging the equation, sales must equal £362 + £35 = **£397**.
13	D	In April expenses were £49 greater than sales: this was the loss. Therefore, expenses must have been £352 + £49 = **£401**.

14	A	In March the sales were £317 but the expenses were £416, thus there was a loss of £99, so the answer is **–£99**.
15	C	In July a profit of £156 was made (£528 – £372). If you add this to the minus bank balance of £57 then a bank balance of **£99** remains.
16	D	The only graph that represents a steady climb to January and then a drop is Graph **D**.
17	B	The volume of the sandpit = $\pi r^2 h$. This gives $3 \times (1.5)^2 \times 0.2$ m, which makes $3 \times 2.25 \times 0.2 = $ **1.35 m³**.
18	D	You need to calculate the circumference of the circle: $\pi d = 3 \times (1.5 + 1.5) = $ **9 m**.
19	C	To find how many drachmas at got to the £, calculate $104\,000 \div 200 = 520$. If you multiply this by 350 you will find how many drachmas George got. $520 \times £350 = $ **182 000**.
20	A	a) 67 500 cm³, b) 60 000 cm³, c) 52 500 cm³, d) 54 000 cm³ – suitcase **A** has the biggest volume.
21	B	James' mean score is obtained by adding up all his scores and dividing by the number of assessments. His scores = 37 but in order to get a mean of 4 over 10 tests his scores must equal 40. Therefore the missing score is $40 – 37 = $ **3**.
22	C	The **range** would give the difference between the highest and lowest score for each applicant. If they were consistent the range would be small; if they were inconsistent the range would be large.
23	C	More people ate **pizza and sausage** on Tuesday than on Thursday.
24	D	A pie chart is a circle of 360 degrees, therefore an item that occupies 90 degrees of the circle represents $90 \div 360$ or $\frac{1}{4}$ or 25% of the total. In this case the total number of people surveyed is 40, and $\frac{1}{4}$ of 40 = **10**.
25	D	Chris could round up to £14, and quickly check his change by calculating **£60 – (4 CDs x £14) = £4**.
26	B	You could dismiss C immediately. If you ignore the bit cut out and multiply length x width to find the area, it is not over 100 cm² so it cannot be correct. Area of A: $(10 \times 12) – (8 \times 4) = $ 88 m². Area of D: $(12 \times 10) – (8 \times 2) = $ 104 m². Area of B: $(12 \times 12) – (5 \times 7) = $ **109 m²**. Therefore **B** is the correct answer.
27	B	300 g of flour makes 20 biscuits. One biscuit requires $300 \div 20 = 15$ g, so to make 55 biscuits calculate $55 \times 15 = $ **825 g**.
28	C	50 g almonds, 150 g sugar and 300 g flour. In order to express this in its simplest form you need to 'cancel' down to the lowest form, in this case divide by 50 = **1 : 3 : 6**.

29	C	By interviewing all the people entering the College, Sam can get a representative sample of students. A would have people travelling all over town, not just to college, B would give the same results, and it's unlikely that they would travel to college from the 'nearest bus stop'. D would be people who use their cars not the bus. **C** is the correct answer.
30	B	10 800 Danish kroner ÷ 12 = £900; 9285 French francs ÷ 10 = £928.50; 2 610 000 Italian lire ÷ 3000 = £870; 2000 Swiss francs ÷ 2.5 = £800. Therefore the **French francs** would be worth most in £s sterling.
31	B	You need to calculate: 4 (days) x 30 (£) plus 125 (miles) x 15 (p) = £(4 x 30) + (125 x 15)p = £120 + 1875p = £120 + £18.75 = **£138.75**.
32	D	$8496 \times \frac{2}{3} = 5664$. You need to calculate 5664 x £15 plus 2832 x £7 = £84 960 + £19 824 = £104 784. Rounded up to the nearest **thousand** pounds this is **£105 000**.
33	C	Reading from the scale: (dish and chicken) 3.8 kg − (dish only) 1.4 kg = (chicken) **2.4 kg**.
34	B	A **pictogram** could be used with images of the pet, for example dog, cat etc., to represent the numbers owned in each category.
35	A	$\frac{1}{6}$ were unable to attend. 120 ÷ 6 = 20; 120 − 20 = 100. Of this 100 there were 20% who did not want to come, therefore 80 people were left. Of this 80, $\frac{1}{8}$ cancelled at the last minute. $\frac{1}{8}$ of 80 is 10 and 80 − 10 = **70**.
36	C	To find out the length of the required zip in centimetres calculate 18 x 2.5 = **45 cm**.
37	C	Maria's domestic refrigerator should be at 3° but is 4° warmer, so it is 7°. A three star rated freezer should be at −18°. The difference in temperature between −18° and 7° = **25°C**.
38	D	Calculate 12.5 metres ÷ 2.5 centimetres. Change to the same unit − 1250 cm ÷ 2.5 cm = 500. The scale the architect needs to work to is **1 : 500**.
39	C	Round up to the nearest metre and nearest pound. The perimeter of the room is (8 + 3) x 2. This gives the quantity of border, x £4 (the cost per roll) = £88. (8 + 3) x 2 x 4 = **£88**.
40	A	Add the parts together: 15 + 12 + 5 = 32 parts. $3200\ cm^3$ of paint are needed for the bedroom. To find out the amount of Ravishing Red, calculate $3200\ cm^3$ ÷ 32 (the parts) = $100\ cm^3$ x 5 (the ratio of Ravishing Red) = **$500\ cm^3$**.

Appendices

A Specification for Application of Number Level 2

B Exemptions from the Key Skills end test

C Where to find out more

D Making connections

KEY SKILLS UNIT

Application of number

What is this unit about?

This unit is about applying your number skills in a substantial activity that involves a series of straightforward tasks.

You will show you can:

- interpret information from different sources;
- carry out calculations;
- interpret results and present findings.

How do I use the information in this unit?

The unit has three parts: what you need to know, what you must do and guidance.

Part **A**
WHAT YOU NEED TO KNOW

This part of the unit tells you what you need to learn and practise to feel confident about applying number skills in your studies, work or other aspects of your life.

Part **B**
WHAT YOU MUST DO

This part of the unit describes the skills you must show. All your work for this section will be assessed. You must have evidence that you can do all the things listed in the bullet points.

Part **C**
GUIDANCE

This part describes some activities you might like to use to develop and show your number skills. It also contains examples of the sort of evidence you could produce to prove you have the skills required.

LEVEL 2

Part A

WHAT YOU NEED TO KNOW

In interpreting information,
YOU NEED TO KNOW HOW TO:

■ obtain relevant information from different sources *(eg from written and graphical material, first-hand by measuring or observing)*;

■ read and understand graphs, tables, charts and diagrams *(eg frequency diagrams)*;

■ read and understand numbers used in different ways, including negative numbers *(eg for losses in trading, low temperatures)*;

■ estimate amounts and proportions;

■ read scales on a range of equipment to given levels of accuracy *(eg to the nearest 10mm or nearest inch)*;

■ make accurate observations *(eg count the number of customers per hour)*;

■ select appropriate methods for obtaining the results you need, including grouping data when this is appropriate *(eg heights, salary bands)*.

In carrying out calculations,
YOU NEED TO KNOW HOW TO:

■ show clearly your methods of carrying out calculations and give the level of accuracy of your results;

■ carry out calculations involving two or more steps, with numbers of any size;

■ convert between fractions, decimals and percentages;

■ convert measurements between systems *(eg from pounds to kilograms, between currencies)*;

■ work out areas and volumes *(eg area of an L-shaped room, number of containers to fill a given space)*;

■ work out dimensions from scale drawings *(eg using a 1:20 scale)*;

■ use proportion and calculate using ratios where appropriate;

■ compare sets of data with a minimum of 20 items *(eg using percentages, using mean, median, mode)*;

■ use range to describe the spread within sets of data;

■ understand and use given formulae *(eg for calculating volumes, areas such as circles, insurance premiums, V=IR for electricity)*;

■ check your methods in ways that pick up faults and make sure your results make sense.

In interpreting results and presenting your findings,
YOU NEED TO KNOW HOW TO:

■ select effective ways to present your findings;

■ construct and use graphs, charts and diagrams *(eg pie charts, frequency tables, workshop drawings)*, and follow accepted conventions for labelling these *(eg appropriate scales and axes)*;

■ highlight the main points of your findings and describe your methods;

■ explain how the results of calculations meet the purpose of your activity.

Part B

WHAT YOU MUST DO

You must:

Carry through at least one substantial activity that includes straightforward tasks for N2.1, N2.2 and N2.3.

Evidence must show you can:

N2.1

Interpret information from **two** different sources, including material containing a graph.

- ■ choose how to obtain the information needed to meet the purpose of your activity;
- ■ obtain the relevant information; and
- ■ select appropriate methods to get the results you need.

N2.2

Carry out calculations to do with:

a amounts and sizes;

b scales and proportion;

c handling statistics;

d using formulae.

- ■ carry out calculations, clearly showing your methods and levels of accuracy; and
- ■ check your methods to identify and correct any errors, and make sure your results make sense.

N2.3

Interpret the results of your calculations and present your findings. You must use at least **one** graph, **one** chart and **one** diagram.

- ■ select effective ways to present your findings;
- ■ present your findings clearly and describe your methods; and
- ■ explain how the results of your calculations meet the purpose of your activity.

Part C

GUIDANCE

Examples of activities you might use

You will have opportunities to develop and apply your number skills during your work, studies or other activities. For example, when:

- carrying out and reporting findings from an investigation or project;
- designing something, measuring up or costing a job;
- following up enquiries from customers or clients.

You will need time to practise your skills and prepare for assessment. So it is important to plan ahead. For example, at least one of your activities must involve following through tasks for N2.1, N2.2 and N2.3. But it is likely you will need to do additional tasks to cover all of Part B.

You can obtain information first-hand by measuring or observing, but you do not have to do this. Your information could come from written sources only. If available, you could use IT to present your findings, but you must show you understand what you have presented.

You will need to think about the quality of your application of number skills and check your evidence covers all the requirements in Part B.

Examples of evidence

2.1 INTERPRET INFORMATION

A description of the substantial activity.

Copies of source material, including the graph, and/or a statement from someone who has checked the accuracy of your measurements or observations.

Records of the information you obtained and the methods you selected for getting the results you needed.

2.2 CARRY OUT CALCULATIONS

Records of your calculations (for a, b, c and d), showing methods used and levels of accuracy. Notes on how you checked methods and results.

2.3 INTERPRET RESULTS
AND PRESENT FINDINGS

Descriptions of your findings and methods. Notes on how the results from your calculations met the purpose of your activity.

At least one graph, one chart and one diagram presenting your findings.

If producing certain types of evidence creates difficulties, due to disability or other factors, you may be able to use other ways to show your achievement. Ask your tutor or superviser for further information.

This unit is for use in programmes
starting from September 2000.

QCA/99/342 First published 1999

Copyright © 1999 Qualifications and Curriculum Authority.

Reproduction, storage, adaption or translation, in any form or by any means, of this publication is prohibited without prior written permission of the publisher, or within the terms of licences issued by the Copyright Licensing Agency. Excerpts may be reproduced for the purpose of research, private study, criticism or review, or by educational institutions solely for educational purposes, without permission, providing full acknowledgement is given.

Printed in Great Britain.

The Qualifications and Curriculum Authority is an exempt charity under the Charities Act 1960.

Qualifications and Curriculum Authority, 29 Bolton Street, London W1Y 7PD. www.qca.org.uk   Chairman: Sir William Stubbs.

Copies of this document may be obtained using the QCA *Publications List and Order Form* or by contacting: QCA Publications, PO Box 99, Sudbury, Suffolk, CO10 6SN. Telephone: 01787 884444, Fax: 01787 378426. When ordering, please quote title and reference number.

B Exemptions from the Key Skills end test

If you have an existing qualification in Mathematics or Application of Number you may not have to sit the end test (Part A). You will, however, still have to produce a portfolio of evidence for Part B.

The qualifications that give exemptions are listed below. You should ask your teachers for further advice and guidance on any exemptions to which you may be entitled.

Part A (External Assessment)

Mathematics[1] and Application of Number

> GCE AS/A Level A-E examination performance provides exemption for the external test in these Key Skills at Level 3.
>
> GCSE A*-C examination performance provides exemption for the external test in these Key Skills at Level 2.
>
> GCSE D-G examination performance provides exemption for the external test in these Key Skills at Level 1.

C Where to find out more

Useful websites

Association of Colleges (AoC)
www.aoc.co.uk

BBC Further Education
www.bbc.co.uk/education/fe
www.bbc.co.uk/education/fe/skills/index.shtml

Department for Education and Employment
www.dfee.gov.uk
If you are involved in producing a Progress File you can gain help from
www.dfee.gov.uk/progfile/index.htm

Further Education Development Agency (FEDA) – the main body leading Key
Skills developments in schools and colleges.
www.feda.ac.uk

For **GNVQ support** try
www.feda.ac.uk/gnvq

National Extension College (NEC) – produces useful material to support Key
Skills development.
www.nec.ac.uk/index.html

Qualifications and Curriculum Authority (QCA) – the organisation responsible for
the development, implementation and quality assurance of all national
qualifications.
www.qca.org.uk

University and Colleges Admissions Service (UCAS)
www.ucas.ac.uk

Letts Educational
www.letts-education.com

D Making connections

If you become familiar with the requirements for the different Key Skills Specifications and their levels, with some thought and planning it is possible to organise your work so that it may be evidence for more than one Key Skill.

Application of Number is the Key Skill that will require you most to adapt or extend your existing work in order to meet the requirements of the specification. Maths coursework is unlikely to be fully acceptable. It may not fulfil the requirements of audience and purpose because you need to apply your number skills to a 'real' problem or situation. Maths coursework that is abstract will not allow you to do this, so seek advice.

Look back at the examples of work in the sample portfolio in Chapter 5. Is there an investigation of a 'real life' problem that you could use your number skills to solve?